The Chinese Family Table

By Kathryn Hulick

MASON CREST

Mason Crest
450 Parkway Drive, Suite D
Broomall, PA 19008
www.masoncrest.com

First printing
9 8 7 6 5 4 3 2 1

Series ISBN: 978-1-4222-4041-0
Hardback ISBN: 978-1-4222-4043-4
EBook ISBN: 978-1-4222-7741-6

Produced by Shoreline Publishing Group LLC
Santa Barbara, California
Editorial Director: James Buckley Jr.
Designer: Tom Carling
Production: Patty Kelley
www.shorelinepublishing.com
Front cover: Asia Images Group/Shutterstock

Library of Congress Cataloging-in-Publication Data Names: Hulick, Kathryn, author. Title: The Chinese family table / by Kathryn Hulick.
Description: Broomall, PA : Mason Crest, 2018. | Series: Connecting cultures through family and food | Includes bibliographical references and index.
Identifiers: LCCN 2017058185| ISBN 9781422240434 (hardback) | ISBN 9781422240410 (series) | ISBN 9781422277416 (ebook)
Subjects: LCSH: Food habits--China--Juvenile literature. | Chinese Americans--Food--Juvenile literature. | China--Social life and customs--Juvenile literature. | United States--Emigration and immigration--Juvenile literature.
Classification: LCC GT2853.C6 H86 2018 | DDC 394.1/20951--dc23 LC record available at https://lccn.loc.gov/2017058185

QR Codes disclaimer:

The Chinese Family Table

by Kathryn Hulick

Contents

KEY ICONS TO LOOK FOR

 Words to Understand: These words with their easy-to-understand definitions will increase the reader's understanding of the text, while building vocabulary skills.

 Sidebars: This boxed material within the main text allows readers to build knowledge, gain insights, explore possibilities, and broaden their perspectives by weaving together additional information to provide realistic and holistic perspectives.

 Educational Videos: Readers can view videos by scanning our QR codes, providing them with additional educational content to supplement the text. Examples include news coverage, moments in history, speeches, iconic moments, and much more!

 Text-Dependent Questions: These questions send the reader back to the text for more careful attention to the evidence presented here.

 Research Projects: Readers are pointed toward areas of further inquiry connected to each chapter. Suggestions are provided for projects that encourage deeper research and analysis.

 Series Glossary of Key Terms: This back-of-the-book glossary contains terminology used throughout this series. Words found here increase the reader's ability to read and comprehend higher-level books and articles in this field.

Introduction

Fireworks crackle in the sky on New Year's Eve. Flashes of white, blue, green, and red dazzle the eyes as loud pops and bangs reverberate through the air. Many cultures around the world set off fireworks to celebrate a variety of holidays. But the tradition got its start in China. The Chinese discovered gunpowder, the concoction that makes fireworks burst, in around 850 CE.

Today, China is the largest country in the world by population. One out of every five people in the world lives there. Chinese culture has a longer history than any other in the world. By 2000 BCE, the ancient Chinese had organized themselves into a society with a single ruler. In addition to gunpowder, the ancient Chinese also invented paper, silk, porcelain, and tea.

The Chinese began to explore the rest of the world as early as 1050 CE. In the 1400s, explorers ventured to Africa and brought back giraffes, among other curiosities. But then new rulers took power. And the Chinese attitude toward leaving home changed. Anyone who left might be labeled a traitor. Chinese rulers restricted or banned emigration, the movement of people to new lands, for several long periods between the 14th and 19th centuries. In the late 17th century, any migrant who returned home risked being put to death.

Even after the law against emigration was lifted, Chinese culture kept most people close to home. This is mainly due to the influence of an ancient scholar called Confucius. His

teachings have shaped the Chinese way of life. Confucianism says that family and loyalty are of utmost importance. Children must obey and care for their parents and other elders. Today, most Chinese maintain a strong attachment to their homeland. They believe in revering their parents and honoring deceased ancestors.

However, as poverty, wars, natural disasters, and changes in government affected various parts of China, caring for family sometimes meant venturing out to foreign lands. Some people left to seek their fortunes elsewhere. Most intended to return home. Even those who stayed abroad maintained very close ties to their family in China. They also continued to cook and eat food from their home regions. Food helped migrants feel at home in faraway lands.

Getting Here

A glint of gold flashed in the banks of a stream. It was 1848, and a workman was building a new sawmill on Sutter's Creek in California. The discovery set off a gold rush that brought tens of thousands of treasure hunters to America. Many of these newcomers were Chinese men. In China, some began referring to the United States as "gold mountain." By 1851, 25,000 Chinese people had moved to California. Gold discoveries in Australia and Canada during the same time period sparked similar waves of migration from China to those countries.

Before the gold rushes, large communities of Chinese people had already

Words to Understand

emigrant   a person who leaves his or her home country to live elsewhere

ethnicity   a person's national or cultural identity

immigrant   a person who has permanently settled in a new country

prejudice   a commonly held opinion about a group of people that is not based on fact or reason

sojourner   a person who temporarily lives in a place

The discovery of gold set off a gold rush that attracted people from around the world, including the first Chinese immigrants to the United States.

settled abroad in nearby countries in Southeast Asia. But the lure of an easy fortune helped spur a migration that eventually established Chinese communities in more far-flung regions of the world.

Many historians do not refer to these early travelers as **emigrants** because they intended to return home after working for several years. A better word for them is **sojourners**. However, most sojourners never actually found work in gold mines. And many never made their way back home. They became **immigrants**, or people who permanently settle in a new country.

Seeking a Fortune Far from Home

Some people, called brokers, made a business out of recruiting male Chinese workers and transporting them abroad. One recruitment notice from the 19th century translates to, "Americans are very rich people. They want the Chinaman to come and make him very welcome. There you will have great pay, large houses, and food and clothing of the finest description." Unfortunately, this was a lie. Life for Chinese sojourners could be extremely difficult. The unluckiest ones wound up trapped as

The hard life and pressure to find work led some men to fall victim to opium abuse.

slaves laboring in horrific conditions in places including Cuba and Peru. Many died.

Luckier sojourners made it to San Francisco, California, and could send mail and money to family back home. But the journey wasn't easy. The culture, landscape, and food were all unfamiliar. One Chinese man wrote of his journey, "When I got to San Francisco I was half starved because I was afraid to eat the provisions [food] of the barbarians." By barbarians, he meant Americans.

 The Chinese in Peru

After slavery was abolished in Peru, plantation and mine owners needed a new source of labor. They found it in China. The Chinese men who came to Peru to work often faced horrific, slave-like conditions. However, as time wore on, Chinese Peruvians began to lift themselves out of poverty and make a better place for themselves in society. Today, five percent of the Peruvian population is of Chinese descent. This has influenced food in the country. Maria Antonieta Zegarra grew up in Peru. She says, "We have Chinese restaurants, which we call Chifa. It's like Chinese food but with Peruvian flavor. It's delicious!"

As the numbers of Chinese living in California increased, though, they established communities complete with groceries selling imported Chinese foods, including tea, rice, bean curd, preserved eggs, and dried fish. They also set up restaurants. White Americans began to visit some of these establishments. In 1851, miner William Shaw wrote that Chinese restaurants were the best places to eat in San Francisco. He said, "The dishes are mostly curries, hashes, and fricassee served up in small dishes and as they are exceedingly palatable [tasty], I was not curious enough to enquire as to the ingredients." Eventually, Chinese men established a reputation as excellent chefs. Many learned how to prepare European dishes and found work as servants cooking for white Americans.

Facing Racism

Despite the success that some Chinese people found, they regularly faced **prejudice** and racism. As early as the 1850s, some white Americans began to spread hateful messages about the Chinese. They viewed them as an inferior race. "They are not of our people and never will be... They do not mix with our people, and it is undesirable that they should,"

In the late 1800s and early 1900s, anti-immigrant feelings grew, including a desire to expel Chinese workers and block future immigration.

stated a racist newspaper column in 1853. After slavery was abolished in the United States in 1865, some Chinese workers took over jobs that had once primarily belonged to African slaves. For example, Chinese men often worked as domestic servants.

Often, the only jobs Chinese workers could find involved difficult,

Where Were the Women?

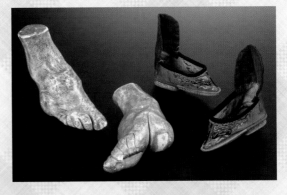

Almost all early Chinese emigrants were young men. In 1850, approximately 4,000 Chinese men lived in San Francisco, but just seven Chinese women lived there. In the male-dominated Chinese society of the time, men ruled the household and provided income. Women did not travel far from the home. In fact, many could not even walk very far due to the practice of foot binding, which has since ended. At the time, tiny feet were seen as a mark of great beauty, but a bound foot could not grow or carry weight properly. However, some Chinese women did make it to America.

In fact, the very first Chinese person known to have come to the United States was a woman named Afong Moy. But she wasn't here freely. Two businessmen brought her over in 1834 to put her on display. Shockingly, people paid 50 cents to see her bound feet, watch her use chopsticks, and listen to her speak Chinese. Decades later, Chinese women living in the United States still aroused curiosity. In rural areas of the Wild West, white neighbors used to call any Chinese woman "China Mary." One "China Mary" worked as a fisher, hunter, prospector, cook, laundry operator, and more in Canada. Another owned a restaurant in Arizona. And a third outlived three husbands and died at the age of 100 in Wyoming.

manual labor. Many opened laundries. One Chinese woman recalls, "In China in the old days women thought that people came over to pick gold. Ai! Really! You think they knew that they were coming to work in the laundry?" Washing and ironing clothes by hand was back-breaking work, and most white Americans weren't willing to do it. Other Chinese immigrants worked in agriculture, doing the difficult labor of preparing fields, planting, or harvesting. Many more Chinese went to work building the Transcontinental Railroad, which connected the east and west coasts of the United States for the first time. The Chinese worked longer hours and received less pay than white men. An estimated 12,000 to 14,000 Chinese men worked on the railroad.

Chinese workers were among the thousands who labored in hot, desert conditions to complete the transcontinental railroad.

Despite these contributions to society, many Americans protested against Chinese labor. In the 1870s, the United States economy wasn't doing well. Many felt that the Chinese were stealing jobs from white Americans. Tensions were especially high in California. J.S. Look lived in the area in the 1870s. He recalls, "Often the small American boys would throw rocks at us." During violent race riots in Los Angeles and San Francisco, angry mobs destroyed Chinese businesses and even killed Chinese people. Then, in 1882, US President Chester Arthur approved

President Chester Arthur signed a law that ended Chinese immigration to America for decades.

a new law that became known as the Chinese Exclusion Act. The law prevented new Chinese workers from entering the United States and made it impossible for Chinese immigrants to become US citizens. This was the first time the United States had ever excluded a group of people based on **ethnicity**; the law remained in effect for many years.

Trapped on Angel Island

Today and during the time of the Exclusion Act, anyone who is born in America automatically becomes a citizen. Two citizens' children, even if those children are born abroad, automatically become citizens, too. So a Chinese man who was born in the United States could bring his children over from China, despite the Exclusion Act. In 1906, a devastating earthquake tore through the city of San Francisco. Many parts of the city were reduced to rubble or burned in fires, including Chinatown. The fires also destroyed birth and citizenship records, and many Chinese immigrants saw an opportunity in this loss. They claimed that they had been born in the United States. Even if this wasn't true, the government had no way to know. Many of these new citizens also claimed to have children, almost all sons, born in China. A business boomed in false paperwork to help young Chinese men emigrate as children of citizens. This got around the restrictions of the Exclusion Act. These immigrants became known as "paper sons."

To help process Chinese immigrants and other people coming into the United States via the Pacific Ocean, the US government opened an immigration center on Angel Island in San Francisco Bay in 1910. This was the

Angel Island history

counterpart of Ellis Island in New York, where streams of immigrants from Europe first arrived. However, on Ellis Island, most immigrants passed through within a few hours. Angel Island was more like a prison. Most Chinese immigrants had to stay there for weeks, months, or even years, trying to prove their identities. L.D. Cio was one of a group of students detained at Angel Island in 1913. He said, "Miserably crowded together and poorly fed, the unfortunate victims are treated by the jailers no better than beasts. The worst is that they are not allowed to carry on correspondence with the outside." Some detainees wrote or carved poetry into the walls. One poem reads, "America has power, but not justice . . . . I bow my head in reflection but there is nothing I can do."

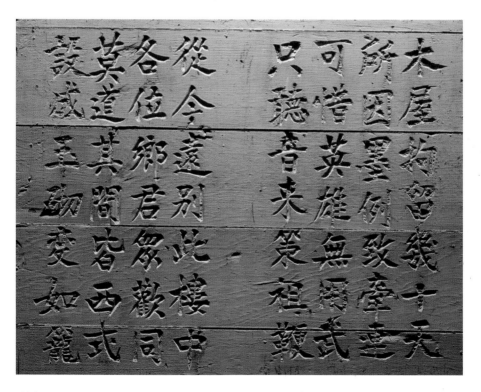

Chinese people stuck on Angel Island inscribed poetry and memories into the walls of the San Francisco Bay buildings.

Fleeing Communism

In 1943, the US government finally ended the Exclusion Act because China was fighting as an ally against the Japanese in World War II. Before, during, and for several years after the war, China was also fighting with itself. Two factions battled off and on for control of the government. In 1949, the communist party finally won, and Mao Zedong took power. Two to three million people fled mainland China. Many of these emigrants were wealthy or powerful people who feared the new government. In her book, *The Chinese in America*, Iris Chang writes, "They sewed gold bullion and jewelry into belts and seams of clothes, even shoes, and shoved their way onto trains so mobbed that people clung to the tops and sides of the railway cars in order to get away."

Taipei is the booming captial of the island nation of Taiwan.

The old government of China relocated to the island of Taiwan, which even today continues to fight for recognition as an independent nation. Many Chinese people also fled to Hong Kong, which was under British control at the time. This city is located on a small island off the southern coast. The advent of communism wound up isolating China from the

Western world. For several decades, very few Chinese people were allowed to leave the country. Most mid-20th century Chinese emigrants came from Hong Kong or Taiwan, not from mainland China.

Looking for Education

In the 1970s and '80s, China began to open up more to the outside world. The Emigration and Immigration Law of 1985 made it much easier for Chinese citizens to leave the country. The number of immigrants from mainland China living in the United States doubled between 1980 and 1990, then doubled again by 2000. As of 2016, 2.1 million Chinese immigrants live in the United States, according to the Migration Policy Institute. Mexico and India are the only nations with larger immigrant populations living in the United States.

The United States is the top destination for Chinese people looking to live, work, or study overseas. Canada and Australia are also popular choices. But the United States' most

Chinese families arrive in countries around the world, often aiming at higher education.

Ivy League universities such as Harvard have seen a large increase in students from many Asian countries, including China.

elite schools, such as Harvard and Yale, carry a prestige that's tough to match elsewhere. China sends more students to study at US colleges and universities than any other nation. While Chinese Americans make up just 0.6 percent of the US population, 20 percent of the students attending elite colleges and universities in the United States are Chinese.

Chinese immigrants who come for higher education typically end up in skilled, high-paying jobs. Many become doctors, scientists, or engineers. Some return to China to pursue careers there, while others remain in the country where they studied. Diana Zhang and her husband both came to the United States for an education. She earned a master's degree and he got a PhD. They had intended to move back to China, but now they have two young boys. "So far, we are staying here," says Zhang. But someday, they may move back. She says, "We haven't settled. Not yet." Her story is similar to that of many other Chinese people in America and other foreign countries. They move for work or an education and then end up staying on to raise a family.

Text-Dependent Questions:

1. Why did the gold rush attract so many Chinese men to California?

2. Why did the United States choose to keep out Chinese workers with the Exclusion Act?

3. What made those who left China after the change to communism different from earlier emigrants?

Research Project:

Look up the history of Chinese immigrants to your city or state. Why did they come to your area? What contributions have they made?

APPETIZER: DIM SUM

China has made snacking into an art form. A meal called "dim sum" consists of many small, bite-size dishes crafted into artful shapes and beautiful presentations.

Dim sum first arose at Chinese tea houses in the Canton region. The owners would sell visitors small snacks to go along with their tea. Over time, these snacks became more and more elaborate, until dim sum became an entire meal. The tradition is now popular around the world. It's often called "Chinese brunch," since dim sum is served from early in the morning through the midafternoon. Diners sit at round tables, and servers push around carts full of dishes. Diners point to what they want. Common dishes include steamed buns, spring rolls, spareribs, sesame seed balls, and desserts such as mango pudding.

Let's Have Tea

"Better to be deprived of food for three days, than tea for one," says an ancient Chinese proverb. As this proverb suggests, tea is central to life in China. The tea plant was originally cultivated in the region. White, green, and black teas all come from the leaves of the same plant. Tea makers process the leaves in different ways to arrive at each variety. Green tea leaves are preserved immediately after picking. Black tea leaves are dried and processed. This increases the concentration of caffeine. The ancient Chinese used tea as a medicine.

Serving tea to another person demonstrates respect or gratitude. Traditionally, children must pour tea for their parents, employees for their bosses, or servants for their masters, and never the other way around. First, a person takes a small sip of the tea. Then he or she takes another sip. Then it's fine to drink. These social traditions have become more flexible recently. But tea remains a very important part of the Chinese identity.

Settling In

When Ye Pei thought about life in Italy, she imagined exploring the arching bridges and deep canals of Venice, which she called "the water city." But the reality of life in Italy was very different. When she arrived in 2011 at the age of 17, she found work at a bar in a town called Solesino two hours from the magical city of Venice. She worked 12 hours every day, seven days a week. After the first week, her hands began to crack, peel, and bleed from the amount of time she spent washing dishes. She struggled with the Italian language, especially with the rolling "r" sound, which doesn't exist in Chinese. Life abroad was a lot harder than she'd

Words to Understand

bilingual able to speak two languages fluently

chopsticks stick-like utensils used to eat, especially in Eastern Asia

cuisine a style of cooking native to a particular country or region

dialect a local variant of a language

vexing difficult or troublesome

wok a round, deep metal frying pan commonly used in Chinese cooking

The beautiful city of Venice, Italy, with its gondolas and canals, presents challenges for Chinese immigrants, even in the 2000s.

thought it would be. But she had an important goal. She wanted to be *lao ban*, a Chinese phrase that means "the boss." As she wrote in her diary, "I will work very hard to learn Italian and to acquire the skills necessary for running a bar. This way Mama and Baba can have an early retirement. This bar has been open for four years and now they are millionaires.... I am not jealous of them because I know one day our family will be even better off. I firmly believe it!"

Pei's modern experience echoes those of early Chinese immigrants. They left home to earn money for their loved ones. They worked grueling jobs with the hopes of a better future for themselves and their families. However, making one's fortune in a new country requires more than just hard work. It requires adjusting to a new culture. A new language, strange social customs, unknown holidays, and weird food all pose a challenge to immigrants. Even wealthy, well-educated Chinese immigrants must come to terms with a cultural divide that may at times seem impossibly vast. Diana Zhang recalls when she arrived in America to study. "In the beginning, it's just happiness—oh, another country! I'm without my parents' control! It's kind of like a honeymoon. Then I suddenly realized everything was different. I felt a little homeless, helpless."

Most Chinese students come to America with some understanding of English.

Language and Letters

Learning a new language is often the first and toughest hurdle that immigrants anywhere in the world face. Without a handle on the local language, it's very difficult to get a job, use public transportation, go shopping, read the news, or otherwise participate in society. For Chinese immigrants to the United States, Canada, Europe, and Australia, the new language is especially **vexing**. English and most European languages all come from the same root, Latin. They mostly use the same alphabet, in which each letter represents a sound. Many European languages also share similar-sounding words.

The Chinese language uses characters, instead of spelling words with letters.

Chinese is completely different. First of all, Chinese is not really one language, but a group of related languages. People from some parts of China cannot understand people from other regions. Mandarin Chinese is the most common version of the language. Most Chinese people today learn Mandarin in addition to their local **dialect**.

In Chinese writing, each symbol, called a character, represents an entire word. Fluent readers of Chinese recognize 40,000 different characters. The spoken language is tonal, meaning that the pitch of the voice can change the meaning, so one sound may represent many different words, depending on the tone used. All of this may appear complicated, but if it's what a person grew up with, it feels normal. "It is so much simpler to just read and write in Chinese," says Pei. She's not alone. Throughout history, many Chinese immigrants have given up trying to learn anything beyond the bare basics of their new homeland's language. It's just too different.

Learning Chinese means memorizing thousands of characters like this one.

Conversely, many children of Chinese immigrants have resisted learning Chinese. They don't understand why they have to master this language that none of their local friends speak. Louise Leng Larson remembers being forced to study Chinese as a child growing up in America in the 1910s. She went to one of many schools that Chinese Americans had established to help carry on their language and culture in their communities. Larson says the lessons were "an ordeal I grew to hate." But when Chinese immigrants and their children do manage to master both languages, everyone benefits. These **bilingual** people help bridge the divide between the East and the West for their neighbors in their new home and for their families back in China.

Round Tables and Chopsticks

American and European foods and eating customs may seem just as alien to new Chinese immigrants as the language. A traditional American or European meal usually involves several courses of food. The guests sit at a rectangular or square table. First, the host sets out

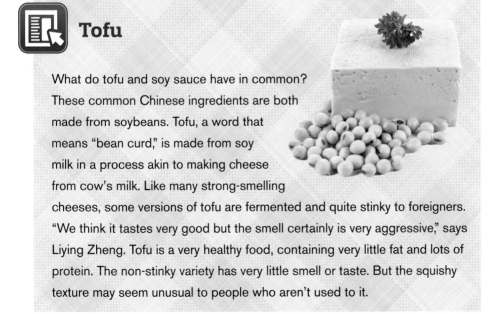

Tofu

What do tofu and soy sauce have in common? These common Chinese ingredients are both made from soybeans. Tofu, a word that means "bean curd," is made from soy milk in a process akin to making cheese from cow's milk. Like many strong-smelling cheeses, some versions of tofu are fermented and quite stinky to foreigners. "We think it tastes very good but the smell certainly is very aggressive," says Liying Zheng. Tofu is a very healthy food, containing very little fat and lots of protein. The non-stinky variety has very little smell or taste. But the squishy texture may seem unusual to people who aren't used to it.

appetizers and drinks. Then everyone enjoys a soup or other first course. Finally, the main dish arrives. Usually, it's a large piece of meat that has baked or simmered for a very long time. People receive their own plates of food and carve up their own meat with a knife and fork.

In China, everything is different, starting with the shape of the table. Chinese people almost always sit at round tables for meals. The food typically all comes out at once. And meat and vegetables aren't often served

 ## Chinese Food in America

Egg rolls, crab Rangoon, teriyaki beef, and General Tso's chicken—these mouth-watering foods show up in take-out containers at Chinese restaurants around America. Yet these foods are nothing like what people in China actually eat.

Chinese food rose in popularity in America because it was cheap, quick, and tasty. Also, Chinese chefs found ways to adapt their native **cuisine** to American tastes. They even invented entirely new dishes. Chef Peng Chang-kuei is credited with popularizing General Tso's chicken. The original dish, he says, was "Hunanese in taste and made without sugar." But in the 1970s, he changed the recipe to appeal to an American appetite. American-Chinese dishes tend to be sweeter and heavier than more authentic Chinese foods. Steamed foods are more common in most areas of China than deep-fried foods such as egg rolls. American-Chinese restaurants also use lots of broccoli, a vegetable that's not native to China. There, chefs use bok choy and other native Chinese veggies.

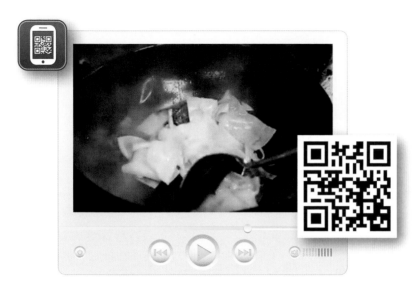

Using a wok

whole. For many dishes, the cook chops foods into small pieces then uses a large, round pan called a **wok** to quickly fry everything. The guests each have a bowl of rice at their places, but they share the communal dishes in the middle of the table, using **chopsticks** to pick up each bite. Tea, as you might expect, accompanies the meal.

China is a large country with a huge range of different cooking and eating styles. Most early Chinese immigrants to America came from the Cantonese region in the south. There, steaming and stir-frying reign supreme. Many meals contain chicken, pork, or beef. The Sichuan region of the southwest uses similar cooking methods and ingredients, but much spicier sauces. Bean curd, called tofu, is popular throughout China, but especially well-loved here. In eastern China, around the city of Shanghai, seafood dishes such as steamed crabs are very popular. People here also enjoy very sweet sauces. All three of these regions serve rice with every meal. However, in northern China, where rice doesn't grow, people eat more

A colorful market in New York City's Chinatown.

noodles, bread, and dumplings. Diana Zhang, who grew up in northern China, points out that the bread here is different from Western bread. "It's steamed instead of baked," she says. Some staples of Chinese cooking are difficult to come by in America and other Western countries. Zhang misses Chinese vegetables the most. However, thanks to the internet, it's easy to order sauces and preserved foods online.

Eating together is such an important part of life that in many parts of China, people don't greet friends or family with "hello." Instead, they ask, "Have you eaten yet?" Familiar food from home helps immigrants feel comfortable when everything else is different. Despite having lived in the United States with her American husband for over 25 years, Lying Zheng still doesn't love American food. "My stomach is still quite Chinese," she says. "You comfort your stomach, you comfort your life."

Text-Dependent Questions:

1. What was Ye Pei's reason for continuing to live and work in Italy?

2. How are Chinese languages different from most European languages?

3. What are three major differences between a Western meal and a Chinese meal?

Research Project:

Look up vegetables native to China. Which do you recognize and which are unfamiliar? Choose one unfamiliar vegetable and research its uses. What familiar vegetable seems most similar? How might you incorporate this Chinese vegetable into a dish you enjoy?

SIDE DISHES: VEGETABLES, MEAT, AND FISH

In a way, almost all Chinese dishes are like Western side dishes. The central component to any meal is rice (or in some regions, noodles). Other foods, including vegetables, meat, and seafood, are served in small bowls or platters for everyone to share. Chinese chefs use a stunning variety of ingredients and cooking methods. One animal, such as a duck or fish, may be cooked whole. Or a chef may prepare a dish from one part of a duck, including the tongue, feet, stomach, wings, neck, or bones. The Chinese also eat pig's blood, hearts, hooves, and other body parts that seem unusual to many foreigners. Many kinds of seafood are popular as well, especially in coastal areas. "In my area, everybody loves jellyfish [picture below]," says Liying Zheng. All of these ingredients may be prepared in numerous ways. Common cooking methods include stir-frying, deep-frying, steaming, blanching, poaching, braising, and roasting, to name just a few. Cold salads and hot soups are also very popular. The ingredients, cooking methods, and flavors used in Chinese dishes vary wildly by region. Within the major regions, communities develop their own unique twists on common dishes.

Legends surround the origin of some popular Chinese dishes. Beggar's chicken is a whole roasted chicken stuffed with pork and vegetables or mushrooms. It takes six hours to prepare. The story goes that a hungry beggar stole a chicken from a farm. The angry farmer chased him, and the beggar quickly buried the chicken in a riverbank. Later, he dug up the bird, which was caked with mud. He roasted it, and the mud hardened to clay. When he knocked the clay off, the chicken was perfectly cooked and delicious. He began preparing chicken this way and selling it. Eventually the emperor tried the dish for himself. The dish represents the idea of rising from poverty into wealth.

Connecting

Ye Pei finally made it to Venice. On her 101st day in Italy, she took a bus and then a train to the city. "It was my dream to come to Venice, and now that I've done it, I feel like I can do anything," she said. "I can reach all my goals one by one, and really make something out of myself here in Italy." Later that year, she passed an Italian language test and received a **residency** card.

As her language improved, she also learned the local culture. For example, she noticed that people in Italy always said "hello," goodbye," and "good morning," even to strangers. So she started doing this too, even though greeting people constantly

Words to Understand

conservative   sticking with traditional values

discrimination   unfair treatment of a particular category of people

exploitative   taking unfair advantage of someone without giving them any benefit

obedience   the trait of following rules or orders

prosperity   wealth or abundance

residency   the place where a person officially lives

Being a tourist is an easy and popular way to connect with other cultures—much easier than becoming a resident.

like that wasn't normal in the region of China where she grew up. One Chinese saying goes, "*Ru jing sui su*," meaning, "Enter a village, follow the customs." Changing one's behavior to fit in with a new culture may feel strange, but in the long run, this helps a newcomer gain acceptance and find success. At the age of 19, just two years after she had arrived in Italy, Pei and her boyfriend bought a bar outside of Verona. She had finally become her own boss.

Obedience or Independence

However, getting used to new social customs isn't always as easy as just saying "hello" more often. Immigrants may never get used to some cultural differences. One of the biggest rifts between American

These US military veterans are all Chinese Americans; they are celebrating at a New York City Veterans' Day event.

and Chinese cultures involves the family and social dynamics. In China, **obedience** is a key virtue. Children are supposed to obey their parents and teachers, and people are expected to follow their bosses and leaders. In America, independence tends to be viewed as more important. Parents expect their grown children to have their own separate lives. And society itself is more loosely structured, with an elected government and free markets. Both Diana Zhang and Liying Zheng mentioned feeling more freedom after moving to the United States. One reason Zhang has stayed is that she feels life will be easier on her two sons. "There, we always had exams, we always studied. Life was tough. I think here seems better. Here they can have more hobbies, in art, sports, and more."

Historically, not all Chinese immigrant parents are so open-minded about how their children should be spending their time. Chinese girls and

Moon Cakes

The Mid-Autumn Festival, also known as the Moon Festival, is an important holiday for Chinese people. During this holiday, people get together with family, look at the full moon, light lanterns, and eat a special food called a moon cake. The cake contains a thick paste or other filling baked inside a lighter crust. All moon cakes are small, round pastries. But they come with a dizzying array of fillings. The most traditional contain bean paste or sesame seed paste, but some contain egg yolks, crayfish, or even bullfrog meat.

women, especially, have faced difficulty trying to break free from cultural traditions. In traditional Chinese culture (as well as in early American culture), women were viewed as inferior to men. A good wife obeyed her husband and cared for the home. In the early 20th century, these **conservative** attitudes toward women and family were beginning to crumble in America. But they persisted for a longer time in China. As a result, Chinese immigrants during the early 20th century often found American women's behavior shocking.

Some Chinese mothers tried to shield their daughters from American culture. They kept their daughters at home doing housework but let their sons play outside. Despite a rigid upbringing, many Chinese women who

Chinatown has been a part of lower Manhattan in New York City since before this image of a funeral procession was taken in 1905.

grew up in the United States demanded more freedom and equal treatment. Many Chinese men didn't like that. One man said, "It is not right for Chinese man born in China to marry Chinese woman born in America . . . They do not have the same training, the same feeling about the home the girls do in China." The role of women in Chinese culture has changed. Today, they can expect more equal treatment both in China and abroad, though they may still face **discrimination** or racism.

Welcome to Chinatown

In the 19th and early 20th century, racist attitudes made it nearly impossible for both male and female Chinese immigrants to fully integrate into a Western community. Especially around the time period of the Exclusion Act, many white Americans did not want to live or work alongside people from China. In 1924, a Chinese woman born in Los Angeles said, "My father told me time and time again that I could never be an American because my skin was yellow and only white people could be Americans." Legally, of course, this was not true. Anyone born in the United States is a citizen. But the racist environment of the early 20th century made even second and third generation Chinese Americans feel unwelcome in their own homeland. Even a college degree didn't help. Stanford University reported in 1928 that it was almost impossible to place Asian college graduates in engineering, manufacturing, or business positions.

To make a place for themselves in such a hostile environment, Chinese immigrants often settled together in their own neighborhood, called Chinatown. On the one hand, these communities helped immigrants band together in the face of oppression. Here, immigrants could rely on each other for jobs, living quarters, friendships, and products and news from home. They could conduct business in their own language, eat familiar foods, and celebrate holidays together. On the other hand, living in Chinatown enforced isolation from American culture on the Chinese people. Some of the biggest and best-known Chinatowns emerged in San Francisco, Los Angeles, New York, Toronto, Canada, and Sydney, Australia.

During the early 20th century, some Chinese people in San Francisco began leading tours of Chinatown. During the Great Depression in the 1930s, Chinatown tourism boomed in cities across the United States. Many of these tours exploited common stereotypes of the Chinese. Some tour organizers paid local people to act out dramas involving crime, enslaved women, and more. Though tourism brought money to Chinatowns, the

This mighty gate signals one of the entrance's to San Francisco's Chinatown, one of the oldest and largest in the West.

business also perpetuated myths about Chinese people and made some residents feel as if their home had become a circus sideshow. "We hated them!" Lung Chin said of the white tourists in New York City's Chinatown. "Because the sightseers, they would come around, they would always be talking bad stories about China."

Exploitative tourism made it more difficult for Chinese people to appreciate Americans and vice versa. But today, most Chinatowns have reinvented themselves as cultural centers that promote cross-cultural communication. Events such as parades, food festivals, and holiday celebrations allow people from all backgrounds to experience China's culture. In this way, Chinatowns can help foster friendships and other connections between Chinese immigrant families and the local community.

 ## A Chinese Take-out Tradition

Today, many American families share a tradition. They eat at a Chinese restaurant or order take-out on Christmas or New Year's Eve. Many believe that the tradition got started because Chinese restaurants were the only ones open for these holidays. Restaurant owner Walter Chan estimates that his restaurant serves 500 pounds of rice and gives out 7,500 fortune cookies on New Year's Eve. Christmas Day is big for business, too. Some Jewish people have made it a tradition to eat Chinese food on December 25th. This most likely began as a way to pass the time on a day that wasn't a holiday for them but was for the majority of Americans.

Time to Celebrate

Holidays offer one of the best opportunities for people of different backgrounds to connect with one another. Liying Zheng married an American man. Her family celebrates Christmas and also Chinese New Year, which usually falls in late January or early February. "Even our Christmas tree has Chinese lanterns on it," she says. On Chinese New Year, they invite many American and Chinese friends and family for a big dinner.

For immigrants from all backgrounds, holidays may bring the greatest feelings of disconnection and homesickness. It's a very lonely feeling to wait for a major holiday to arrive, then realize that no one around shares in the excitement. Pei missed celebrating Chinese New Year during her first year in Italy because she had to work. Many Chinese people, no matter how far they have traveled, try to return home for Chinese New Year.

Chinese New Year traditions

They call the holiday the Spring Festival. People decorate their windows and doors with red paper lanterns and Chinese phrases for good fortune. Parents give their children red envelopes full of money. The color red symbolizes happiness and **prosperity**. Families make dumplings filled with ground meat and vegetables. Their shapes represent ancient Chinese money. Sticky rice cakes mean that the family will stick together. Long noodles stand for a long life. And fish represent surplus, because in Mandarin, the two words have the same pronunciation.

And of course, no Chinese New Year celebration would be complete without fireworks. During Pei's second year in Italy, she got to celebrate the holiday with her family and a group of other Chinese immigrants. As she watched the fireworks, she got as excited as she had the day she finally made it to Venice.

Text-Dependent Questions:

1. Why might an immigrant or child of immigrants feel as though he or she doesn't belong anywhere?

2. What family values are more common in Chinese culture than in American culture?

3. How do most Chinese families celebrate Chinese New Year?

Research Project:

Plan a Chinese New Year party. Look up a recipe for a traditional food to serve. Decide how to decorate, and find one historical reason for each type of decoration. Write out a description of the holiday and its meaning for your guests.

MAIN DISH: RICE

When Ye Pei traveled to Italy, she brought a rice cooker in her luggage. In one of her language classes, the Italian teacher asked her Chinese students what they might eat for breakfast, lunch, and dinner. The answer to all three questions was the same: "rice." The teacher was surprised. "You guys always have rice, even in the morning?" The students tried to explain that they needed to eat rice. It was the only food that could give them the energy they needed to get through the work day. Yogurt, apples, or bread just wouldn't do it.

Rice forms the central component of almost all Chinese meals. People from northern China may serve noodles or bread in place of rice, but everywhere else, rice is always the main dish. The meat, fish, vegetables, and other foods on the table complement the rice. A pot of rice alone can serve as a complete meal if necessary. But a meal without rice? That's hard for many Chinese people to imagine. Mary Tsui Ping Yee recalls a few weeks during World War II when rice supplies ran out in her town in Pennsylvania. Every time her mother served potatoes, bread, or noodles, she said unhappily, "No rice to eat." Yee explains what her mother meant: "This is really not a meal; without rice, it's only a snack!"

The true significance of rice is difficult for anyone who's not Chinese to grasp. Liying Zheng explains that the Chinese use the phrase "rice bowl" to refer to jobs. An "iron rice bowl" is a secure job. When a person loses a job, he or she has a "broken rice bowl." Zheng says, "Rice means everything. It's life to a lot of people." To Western eaters, fried rice is a regular part of Chinese meals.

Reaching Back

Being in a new country surrounded by a new language and culture changes a person in subtle and long-lasting ways. Ye Pei's uncle, who had immigrated to Italy several decades before Pei, had no desire to go back to China. He said, "The Italians see me as Chinese. But the Chinese see me as a foreigner." This feeling of not really belonging anywhere affects almost all immigrants and their families. There are two ways to respond. Some people work even harder to fit in, while others cling to their old ways, spending more time with fellow immigrants than with local people. Most eventually find a balance in which they can be part of both cultures.

Words to Understand

assimilate   to adapt or adjust to a new place, idea, or culture

stereotype   a commonly held belief about a group of people that is not based on reason

Connecting with family and friends back home in China has become remarkably easy with the rise of cell phones and email.

Between Two Worlds

No matter how hard an immigrant tries to **assimilate** into the local culture, the locals may continue to see that person as an outsider. For Chinese immigrants to Western countries, race has unfortunately made it especially difficult to feel a sense of belonging. Even second or third generation Chinese Americans who speak fluent English and follow American social customs may encounter prejudice simply because they aren't white. Racism against the Chinese and other Asians is less out in the open today than it was during the period surrounding the Exclusion Act. But it's still out there. A 2012 report from AAPI Nexus found that Asian American students experience bullying—in person and online—more than any other ethnic group.

Often, racism against Asian Americans takes the form of others assuming that a person who is Asian is not really American. For example, when US figure skater Michelle Kwan came in second after a white teammate in the 1998 Olympics, one media outlet reported, "American beats Kwan." In

Chinese American Michelle Kwan was an Olympic star for the United States.

fact, both skaters were Americans. That same year, Matt Fong was running for a seat in the US Senate. A reporter asked whether he would support China or the United States if war broke out between the two nations. Fong's family had been in the United States for four generations. Yet his loyalty was still called into question. Author Iris

Matt Fong was a prominent politician and Senate candidate in California.

Chang writes, "How many hoops do we have to jump through to be considered 'real' Americans?"

The result of this type of treatment is that children and grandchildren of Chinese immigrants may not feel completely welcome in the very place they call home. Complicating things even further, some descendants come from a mixed background, where one parent is Chinese but the other is white, black, or from another Asian country. This may make it even more likely for others to question whether the person is a "real" American. When someone asks Cy Wong, "Who are you and where are you from?" He responds, "I am a descendant of an African native, a Chinese native, and a native American Indian. But my nativity is American." He feels that he is American—and that's more important than any particular part of his complex cultural heritage.

The stereotype of a great Asian student has placed perhaps an unfair burden on Asian Americans of all backgrounds.

Some children who face confusion about their identity may try to break away from the parents' culture (or cultures). They may stop speaking their parents' language or eating their traditional foods. They may also rebel against aspects of a specific culture, such as the idea that Chinese children must be perfectly obedient and excel in school. Conversely, they may try to be a perfect child, believing that in perfection they will gain acceptance.

The Best and the Brightest?

Beginning in the 1980s, a new **stereotype** began to emerge about Chinese Americans and Asian Americans in general. People started to expect that students from these backgrounds would perform well in school. During this period, wealthy Chinese and Taiwanese families had begun sending their children to top private schools and universities in the United States. These children's families usually placed a lot of pressure on them. The students often felt that they had to excel or they would disappoint their parents. In the 1980s, a professor at California State University discovered a joke circulating among his Taiwanese American students that listed how to be a perfect Taiwanese kid. Here were some of the items on the list: "Score 1600 on the SAT. Play the violin or piano on the level of a concert performer. Apply to and be accepted by 27 colleges. Have three hobbies: studying, studying, and studying."

The stereotype spread. Today, according to Pew Research Center, more than 70 percent of Americans describe Chinese people as "hardworking, competitive, and inventive." It seems positive to call out the successes of a

More than 350,000 people from Taiwan have moved permanently from their home country (above) to the United States.

group of people, but stereotyping Chinese students as especially brilliant covers up the inequalities that these students continue to face. In addition, the stereotype means that Chinese students may face much higher expectations from their parents and teachers than do their classmates from other ethnic backgrounds. These expectations may be unreasonable or unfair.

A New Name

Chinese students aren't all especially smart. But it's true that Chinese culture places a lot of emphasis on education. According to a report by a Chinese online education institution, Chinese students spend an average of three hours on homework each day. Today in China, learning English is an important goal for most students. Since English

Fortune Cookies

Americans know what to expect at the bottom of any Chinese take-out bag: a handful of fortune cookies. Each sweet, crunchy cookie contains a thin strip of paper bearing a message. However, these cookies are not really Chinese. They first appeared in California in the early 1900s.

This is your lucky day!

Most historians believe that Japanese immigrants first started selling the cookies. The source of inspiration may have been fortunes written on slips of paper at Japanese Buddhist temples. Some temples sell cookies with fortunes baked inside. But Chinese restaurants made the idea famous.

Chinese-American food museum exhibit

has become the international language of business, they will likely need English communication skills to succeed in their careers. Beginning in the 1990s, many of these English-language learners also began adopting English names, even if they never intended to study, work, or live in an English-speaking country. Many of these students believe it will be easier for Western business partners and colleagues to pronounce or remember an English name.

Many Chinese immigrants choose to use English first names as well. They also usually get in the habit of saying their family name second. In China and other parts of Asia, people say their names the other way around, with the family name first.

Diana Zhang decided to go by the name "Diana" because people constantly mispronounced her Chinese name, "Di" (DEE). Her two sons both have Chinese names, but they are also hard for Westerners to pronounce. So in America she uses their English names instead. Writer Huan Hsu believes that this phenomenon reveals yet another cultural difference. "In the United States, people tend to view names and identities as absolute things... but in China, identities are more amorphous [flexible or shape-changing]." It's more common in China for people to change their names or use multiple names. So it shouldn't come as a surprise that many Chinese immigrants choose to use English names to fit in.

Returning Home

A new name may help make an immigrant's transition slightly easier. But it could take years or even generations for a family to truly feel at home in a new country. Regular visits back to China can help rejuve-

The busy Beijing Airport is first stop for many Chinese returning home.

Small Differences

Diana Zhang has noticed many small differences between life in America and life in China. Each one has required some adjustment for her and her family. For one thing, she says Americans tend to wear more casual clothes, while Chinese people like to dress up more. "Every time we go home, we buy a lot of clothes," she says. In addition, she has noticed that Americans like to divide up a room using furniture. But to her, it's more normal to put everything against the walls and corners, leaving a

big space in the center. And this is how she set up her home in the United States. Finally, she says that in America, "Without a car, you couldn't go anywhere." In China, especially in the cities, public transportation is much more easily available than it is in America.

nate a person who's feeling the pressure of adjusting to a new language and customs. Or, these visits can help remind later generations of their heritage. Liying Zheng's son goes to China to visit family every other year. But not everyone is able to afford long trips back and forth. Thankfully, today's technology has made it easier than ever to stay connected with a faraway homeland. Chinese immigrants use social media, video calls, and texts to keep up with family back home. When Diana Zhang can't be with her family in China for a holiday, they send photos of their celebrations.

Some Chinese immigrants do not intend to stay abroad. They may fuel their days with dreams of returning home for good. Today, many young Chinese people leave to earn an education in a Western nation, but plan to return to China to work. While many follow through with their plans to return to China, others never do. They may find a job in the new country or start a family. Throughout their lives, these unintentional immigrants may continue to imagine returning to China. Victor Wong grew up in San Francisco's Chinatown during the 1930s. He remembers, "The older people, they were always talking about going back home. All the time. 'When we go back to China we'll have this and we'll have that; there won't be any more discrimination.'"

But many immigrants find that returning home after an extended period living abroad isn't what they imagined. The place they left behind is never exactly how they remember it. And they themselves have changed, too. Flora Belle Jan, a Chinese American woman born in California, moved to China in 1932 with her husband. Jan had always dreamed

Chinese food has taken a permanent place in the American diet.

of living in China. But once there, she couldn't make friends. She didn't read or write Chinese. She cooked American food for her children and bought them Western clothing.

Immigration transforms people. Over the generations, an immigrant family takes on more and more of the habits and traditions of the new culture. But most families strive to keep their cultural heritage alive. One of the best ways to do this is through food. Family recipes handed down through the generations bring back the smells and tastes of an ancient homeland, and remind people of the places their ancestors left behind, seeking a better life for their families.

Text-Dependent Questions:

1. What is an example of racism that a Chinese American person might face today?

2. Why do many Chinese students take on English names?

3. How might a trip home to China turn out differently than an immigrant expects?

Research Project:

Look into your own family history. What cultures are part of your family's past? How do these cultures affect your family's lifestyle and celebrations? How would you describe your cultural identity? What makes you feel proud of the culture or cultures that you identify with?

DESSERT

Dessert is not really a part of Chinese food culture. People do cook and eat sweet dishes, but they are often served alongside the rice and everything else. For example, a meal might include sugar-coated cooked fruit or steamed buns with a sweet filling. Red bean paste is a common ingredient in Chinese sweet foods. Since red is the color of Chinese New Year, this paste is a staple in sweet foods served during the holiday. It shows up inside sesame seed balls, pancakes, or dumplings. During the Mid-Autumn Festival, moon cakes are everywhere. Again, these are typically eaten as snacks or during a meal, not afterwards. Sticky rice (pictured below) is another popular Chinese sweet food. Liying Zheng remembers eating it as a snack when she was a child. "Every afternoon between lunch and dinner, [our nanny] would serve a plate full of sticky rice," she recalls. Thanks to the influence of Western culture, some Chinese families have gotten used to eating cake and ice cream after a meal on special occasions. But traditionally, if Chinese people eat anything after a meal, it's just a platter of fresh fruit.

RECIPE

Tomato and Egg Stir Fry
(xi hong shi chao ji dan 西红柿炒鸡蛋)

Ingredients:
- 1 1/2 tablespoons vegetable oil
- 4 eggs, beaten
- 1 carrot, sliced
- 2 large tomatoes, chopped
- 1 green onion, chopped
- 1 teaspoon salt
- Steamed rice to serve with

Preparation:

1. Heat 1 tablespoon vegetable oil in a medium-size skillet or wok over medium-high heat.

2. When the oil is hot, add eggs and cook until the bottom side is done but the top is still raw, about 30 seconds. Stir with a spatula, chopping the egg into bite-size pieces, until the egg is just cooked. Turn to the lowest heat, transfer the egg to a plate, and set aside.

3. Add the remaining 1/2 tablespoon of oil and carrot and turn back to medium-high heat. Stir the carrot until fragrant.

4. Add tomato and the green onion and stir fry until the edges are slightly charred and the texture becomes soft, about 1 minute.

5. Add the egg back into skillet and sprinkle with salt. Quickly mix everything together with a spatula until evenly seasoned.

6. Serve over steamed rice.

Serves 2-4

Find Out More

Books

Chang, Iris. *The Chinese in America: A Narrative History.* New York: Viking Press, 2003.

Ma, Suzanne. *Meet Me in Venice: A Chinese Immigrant's Journey from the Far East to the Faraway West.* Lanham, MD: Rowman & Littlefield, 2015.

Mendelson, Anne. *Chow Chop Suey: Food and the Chinese American Journey.* New York: Columbia University Press, 2016.

Teitelbaum, Michael. *Chinese Immigrants.* New York: Facts on File, 2005.

Websites

https://www.migrationpolicy.org/article/chinese-immigrants-united-states
Learn more about the history of Chinese immigration to the United States here.

https://www.migrationpolicy.org/programs/data-hub/charts/immigrant-and-emigrant-populations-country-origin-and-destination
This interactive map shows how many Chinese immigrants have settled in countries around the world.

http://aus.thechinastory.org/archive/chinese-immigration-to-australia-and-chinese-australians/
Discover the history of the Chinese in Australia on this website.

https://www.thespruce.com/chinese-4128473
Find authentic Chinese recipes and learn the history behind popular dishes on this website.

https://myimmigrationstory.com/
It's not just Chinese immigrants who have contributed to America's rich culture. Read personal stories about immigrants from all over the world at this site.

Series Glossary of Key Terms

acclimate   to get used to something

assimilate   become part of a different society, country, or group

bigotry   treating the members of a racial or ethnic group with hatred and intolerance

culinary   having to do with the preparing of food

diaspora   a group of people who live outside the area in which they had lived for a long time or in which their ancestors lived

emigrate   leave one's home country to live in another country

exodus   a mass departure of people from one place to another

first-generation American   someone born in the United States whose parents were foreign born

immigrants   those who enter another country intending to stay permanently

naturalize   to gain citizenship, with all its rights and privileges

oppression   a system of forcing people to follow rules or a system that restricts freedoms

presentation   in this series, the style in which food is plated and served

Index

Photo Credits

Author Bio

Kathryn Hulick is a freelance writer and former Peace Corps volunteer. For two years, she lived in Kyrgyzstan, a small country that borders China and Russia. There, she experienced first-hand what it's like to try to get used to a new language, culture, and foods. She ate a lot of mutton and potatoes! When she returned to the United States, she started writing for children. Her books include: *Hydrogen* and *Gold* in the Chemistry of Everyday Elements series and *My Teenage Life in Russia*. She also contributes regularly to *Muse* magazine and the Science News for Students website. She enjoys hiking, painting, reading, and working in her garden. Learn more about her work at kathrynhulick.com.